Dublin City Parks
&
Gardens

Dublin City Parks
&
Gardens

MOIRA BOWERS

THE LILLIPUT PRESS
DUBLIN

First published 1999 by
THE LILLIPUT PRESS LTD
62–63 Sitric Road, Arbour Hill, Dublin 7, Ireland

A CIP record for this title is available from the British Library

ISBN 1 901866 29 7

The Lilliput Press receives financial assistance from An Chomhairle
Ealaíon / The Arts Council of Ireland.

Set in 11 on 14 Sabon with Univers Light display headings

Printed and bound in Ireland by Colour Books of Baldoyle, Dublin

For my parents, David and Diana, with love

Contents

Acknowledgments

The author and publisher wish to thank Dublin Corporation and Dúchas, The Heritage Service of the Department of Arts, Heritage, Gaeltacht and the Islands, for their support of this publication.

Maps

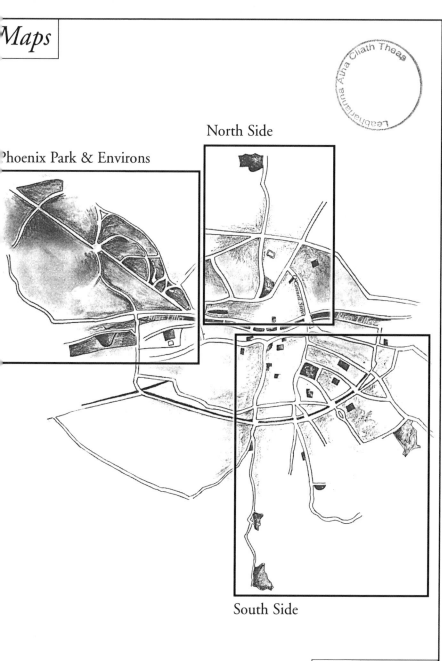

Phoenix Park & Environs

North Side

River Liffey

River Liffey

South Side

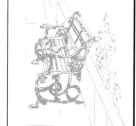

Phoenix Park & Environs

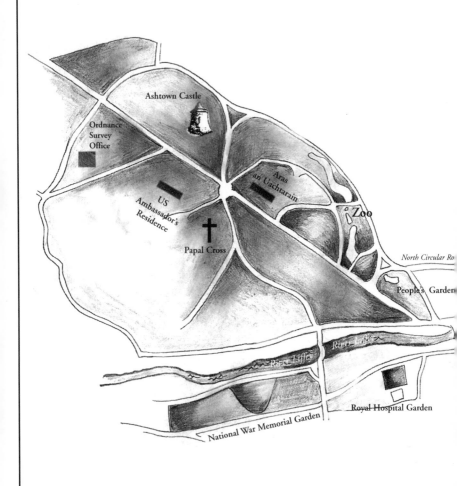

Ashtown Castle

Ordnance
Survey
Office

Aras
an Uachtarain

Zoo

US
Ambassador's
Residence

North Circular Ro

Papal Cross

People's Garden

River Liffey

River Liffey

Royal Hospital Garden

National War Memorial Garden

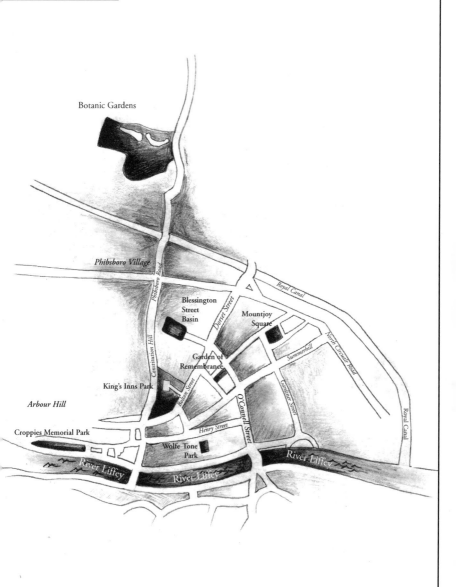

Botanic Gardens

Phibsboro Village

Royal Canal

Blessington
Street
Basin

Dorset Street

Mountjoy
Square

Summerhill

North Circular Road

Constitution Hill

Phibsboro Road

Garden of
Remembrance

King's Inns Park

Bolton Street

Arbour Hill

Capel Street

O'Connell Street

Royal Canal

Croppies Memorial Park

Henry Street

Wolfe Tone
Park

River Liffey

River Liffey

River Liffey

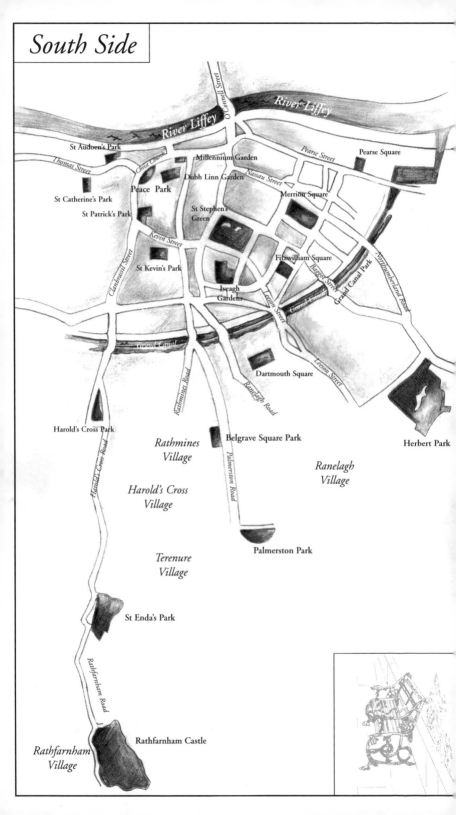

Dublin City Parks
&
Gardens

Phoenix Park

Phoenix Park is the largest enclosed city park in Europe. It comprises one thousand seven hundred and fifty-two acres within a seven-mile circumference, and its nine gates are interlinked by a network of roads, the main one being Chesterfield Avenue which runs straight from Parkgate Street north-west to Castleknock.

The park was created in 1662, but the history of the land on which it stands can be traced back to the twelfth century, when the first Baron of Castleknock ceded lands both north of the Liffey (including what is now Phoenix Park), and south as far as Kilmainham, to the Knights of St John of Jerusalem, an order devoted to helping the poor and sick.

In 1542, following the dissolution of the monasteries by Henry VIII, the lands were confiscated by the Crown. They were later sold to a Sir Edward Fisher, who built a country house on Thomas's Hill, where the Magazine Fort now stands. This was called 'Phoenix House'. The name is thought to have derived not from the mythological bird of

the same name, but from a corruption of the Gaelic 'fionn uisce' (clear water), on account of there being a spring of water close by.

In 1611 Fisher sold his property back to the Crown for use by its representative in Ireland as a summer residence, away from the uncongenial seasonal stench surrounding the State Apartments at Dublin Castle, which was caused by the medieval city's lack of sanitation.

However, it was not until James Butler, Duke of Ormonde, became Lord Lieutenant in 1662 that the land was developed into a real park, which Ormonde enclosed and stocked with fallow deer from England. Further enhancements were made by Lord Chesterfield, who was viceroy between 1744 and 1747. He built roads and paths, erected the Phoenix Monument, and, in 1747, opened the grounds to the public.

Further landscape improvements were carried out between 1832 and the 1840s under Decimus Burton, landscape designer and architect. He designed the park's gate-lodges, and, with the design of London Zoo (1826) already to his credit, he built the Zoological Gardens in Phoenix Park between 1831 and 1832.

Among the park's monuments is the Wellington Obelisk, which, at some two hundred and five feet, is Ireland's highest column. It was built between 1817 and 1861, to commemorate the Duke of Wellington, victor of Waterloo, who was born in Dublin. The Papal Cross, which stands on the edge of the Fifteen Acres, is approximately one hundred and fifteen feet in height. It commemorates the visit of Pope John Paul II to Ireland in September 1979.

The park is home to Aras an Uachtaráin, formerly the Viceregal Lodge, designed by Nathaniel Clements and built between 1751 and 1752. It served as the lord lieutenant's residence until 1922, and after the establishment of the Free State it became the residence of the governor general. In 1938 Dr Douglas Hyde took up residence there as the first President of Ireland, and since that time it has remained the official residence of the president.

Ashtown Castle dates back to the early seventeenth century. It was incorporated into the Under-Secretary's Lodge, and later became the Apostolic Nunciature. It currently houses the Phoenix Park Visitor Centre.

Other buildings in the Park include the Ordnance Survey Office, the Magazine Fort, St Mary's Hospital, the United States Ambassador's Residence, the Civil Defence Headquarters, the Garda Headquarters, and the Army Headquarters.

The Park is currently organized into four zones. The 'Special Use Zone' comprises areas enclosed for park management or institutional purposes, to which public access is prohibited or restricted, or, as in the case of the Zoological Gardens, subject to charge.

The 'Passive Recreation Zone' includes the greater area of the park, and is suitable for walking and wildlife-watching.

The 'Intensive Recreation Zone', situated mainly at the eastern end of the park, includes areas of important historic landscape interest. Active sports are also provided for within this zone.

The 'Natural Zone', in the north-west corner, includes a nature trail, and gives priority to wildlife conservation within a natural habitat. Listings of wild flowers were first made in the park in 1726 by Caleb Threlkeld, and today many of those same plants can be found, such as gypsywort, ladies' tresses, orchid, and burnet saxifrage.

Trees cover 30 per cent of the park's surface. There are special specimen trees, ceremonial trees, tree-lined avenues and woods. The specimen trees include a giant redwood, native of the Sierra Nevada in California, which can be found close to Ashtown Castle. An example from among the ceremonial trees, planted to commemorate particular events, is a pendunculate oak (*Quercus robur*) planted by Pope John Paul II in the formal garden of Aras an Uachtaráin. In 1998, 250 oak saplings were planted to commemorate two and a half centuries of the park's existence.

Chesterfield Avenue, the park's main thoroughfare, is stagger-lined with beech, lime and horse chestnut trees. 'Oldtown', lying between the U.S. Ambassador's Residence and the Ordnance Survey office, is the most extensive of the woods. It is made up predominantly of hawthorn, ash and oak. Among the other woods is Sankey's, which derives its name from Hierome Sankey, a soldier in Ormonde's army, while Bishops Wood has been incorporated into the Peoples' Flower Garden (opened in 1864).

Deer Keeper's Lodge

Wildlife found in the park ranges from ducks, swans, butterflies and six species of bat, to grey squirrels, foxes, otters, rabbits, shrews, hedgehogs, and, of course, the herd of fallow deer, which currently numbers over five hundred. The best time to catch a glimpse of the deer is at five o'clock in the morning, when they can usually be found in the vicinity of the Papal Cross.

Over the centuries, Phoenix Park has borne witness to a staggering range of human activities and events.

In the eighteenth century, bare-knuckle boxing was all the rage at Donnelly's Hollow near the site of the Wellington Monument, while wrestling contests were held on Sunday mornings at the Nine Acres. There are reports, too, of one 'Sambo the Black' and 'Jack the Tumbler' performing acrobatics 'to the amusement of thousands'.

The nineteenth century was marked by the infamous Phoenix Park Murders of Saturday 6 May 1882. Lord Frederick Cavendish, Chief Secretary for Ireland, and his under-secretary, T.H. Burke, were killed almost directly opposite the Viceregal Lodge, as they were walking home in the evening, by members of a group called the Invincibles. Although the incident had been observed from the windows of the Viceregal Lodge, it was dismissed as a drunken skirmish. The truth was not discovered until it was too late.

At the request of Lord Cavendish's wife, no monument was erected to honour the memory of the murdered men, but today they are remembered by two small wayside crosses cut out of the grass embankment where they died.

During the Second World War the park was used for the storage of coal and turf, and wire was slung across the Chesterfield Road to prevent stray German aircraft from using it as a landing strip.

Currently, Phoenix Park is maintained by Dúchas. In 1986 it was designated a National Historic Park.

Opening Hours: Open to the public at all times, except for the People's Garden (Parkgate entrance), which opens at 10.30 Monday to Saturday and 10.00 Sunday, and closes between 16.00 in December and January and 21.30 in June and July.

PHOENIX PARK VISITOR CENTRE
January – mid-March: Saturday – Sunday 9.30–16.30
mid–end March: 9.30–17.00 daily
April – May: 9.30–17.30 daily
June – September: 10.00–18.00 daily
October: 9.30–17.00 daily
November – December: Saturday – Sunday 9.30–16.30
Last admission 45 minutes before closing.

Facilities include: 'Phoenix Park through the Ages', a 21-minute audio-visual presentation. Tel.: (01) 6770095 Fax: (01) 8205584

Buses: 66, 66A, 67, 67A, 25, 25A from Middle Abbey Street to Parkgate Street; 37, 38, 39 from Middle Abbey Street to Ashtown Cross Gate; 10 from O'Connell Street to North Circular Road Gate

Nearby: Kilmainham Gaol, Irish Museum of Modern Art, Royal Hospital Garden, National War Memorial Garden

National War Memorial Garden

We have found
safety with all things
Undying, the winds and morning.
Tears of men and mirth.
The deep night
And birds singing,
And clouds flying,
And sleep, and freedom,
And the autumnal earth.
—Rupert Brooke, 1914 (inscribed on the floor of the folly
at the beginning of the path into the garden)

The National War Memorial Garden at Islandbridge
commemorates the 49,400 Irish servicemen who lost
their lives in the First World War, and in recent years has
also been used as the site of commemorations of the Second World War, in which some 8000 Irishmen were
killed.

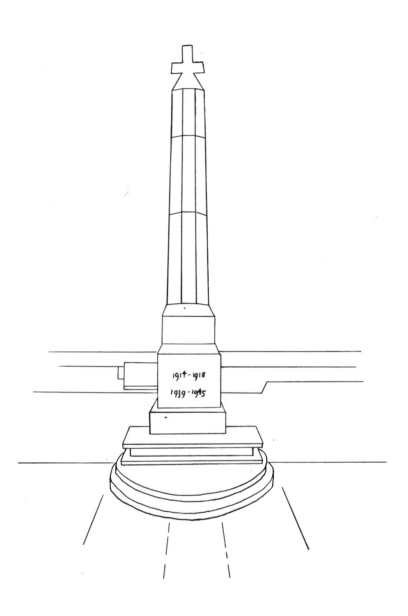

[26]

The plan to create a memorial garden was initiated in 1919 through a committee headed by Sir Dunbar Plunket Barton. It was not until December 1931, however, that agreement was reached to begin work on the garden, to the specifications of the architect Sir Edwin Lutyens. It took more than six years to complete.

A memorial cross at the top of an imposing semi-circular flight of steps, a tomb to the unknown warrior, fountains, and four 'book rooms' (two on each side) adorn the garden, and beyond them are two sunken rose gardens. The cross and tomb are said to symbolize a cross on its high altar, while the fountains on either side of the tomb represent the altar's candlesticks, and the fountain's water represents candle grease.

Five hundred war veterans – half of them Irish and half British – were employed on the construction of the Garden. Working mostly by hand, they excavated some one hundred thousand tons of soil to create the site. The tomb weighs seven and a half tons while the imposing Memorial Cross is in eight large sections. Much of the granite with which the memorial structures were built came from Barnaculla, County Dublin, and Bally-knockan, County Wicklow.

The book rooms, representing the four Irish provinces, were built to house Ireland's Memorial Records. These eight volumes contain the names of the Irish dead from the First World War, in alphabetical order. They are illustrated in black and white by Harry Clarke.

One of the book rooms houses the famous Ginchy Cross, made in December 1916 by the Pioneer Battalion of the 16th Irish Division from a beam of a shattered farmhouse in Flanders. This had been placed between the villages of Ginchy and Guillemont on the Somme battlefield in 1917, and remained there for nine years. However, because it is illegal in France to erect monuments on pastureland, it was brought back to Ireland in 1937, while a permanent granite cross was erected in a Ginchy churchyard.

Unfortunately, over the years, the Garden fell into neglect and suffered from vandalism. In the early 1980s, through a combined effort of the Office of Public Works and the National War Memorial Committee, at the instigation of an ex-Irish Guardsman, Campbell Heather, the concept of a permanent, well-tended Memorial Garden was resuscitated. Restoration work is now complete, and the Garden today is officially managed by Dúchas in co-operation with the National War Memorial Committee.

In 1995, on the fiftieth anniversary of the end of the Second World War, history was made when the ceremony at the cenotaph was attended for the first time not only by the Irish Taoiseach but by the Vice President of Sinn Féin, as well as by representatives of the Irish army and the British government, indicating a unity among men of all factions together to honour their dead.

Opening Hours: Monday–Friday 8.00 until dark
Saturday–Sunday 10.00 until dark

Guided tours available on request. Tel: (01) 6613111 (Head Office) or (01) 6770236 (Gardens)

Buses: 51 and 61 from Aston Quay

Nearby: Kilmainham Gaol, Irish Museum of Modern Art, Royal Hospital Garden, Phoenix Park

---

Kilmainham Hospital Garden

There's something grandiose about this garden which, viewed from a height, resembles a mosaic or neatly woven tapestry. Extending to five acres, its geometric proportions echo the square, classical symmetry of the Kilmainham Hospital building, designed by the architect Sir William Robinson and built between 1680 and 1684.

The style of both building and garden reflects the social ethos of the time. Following the two civil wars in England (1642–6 and 1648–51) of King Charles I's reign, and Cromwell's government (1651–8), the restoration of Charles II to the throne in 1660 ushered in a new era of peace. This was reflected in society by a desire for stability, and in the arts by the embrace of classicism with its characteristic balance and harmony.

The era was marked, too, by a taste for French architecture. The Lord Lieutenant of Ireland, the Duke of Ormonde, who had spent time with the exiled Charles II in Paris, returned to Dublin with a heightened awareness and appreciation of continental art. The design of Kilmainham Hospital is influenced by Louis XIV's Hôtel des Invalides in Paris, while Kilmainham's formal 'vista' garden is reminiscent of that at the Palace of Versailles.

Kilmainham Hospital was completed in 1684 to house veteran soldiers. It predates by two years its sister building, the Royal Hospital in London, home of the red-coated Chelsea pensioners, designed by Sir Christopher Wren. In the 1920s it was converted into a Garda headquarters, and later it became a museum store. By the 1980s the whole area had suffered a decline, and only reverted to a high standard of upkeep when the Office of Public Works restored the property. The Hospital is now a centre for the arts and culture, and it houses the Irish Museum of Modern Art.

In the once-derelict grounds, a classical vista garden, with its terrace, parterre and wilderness areas, has been re-created in the spirit of the late seventeenth century. Kilmainham's parterre, designed to be viewed from an elevated terrace, was planted along traditional lines in 1988 with box hedging (*Buxus sempervirens*), evenly spaced ball-shaped hollies (*Ilex argentea automarginata*) and triangular topiary yews (*Taxus baccata*). Ornamental trees in white-painted boxes also decorate the lawns.

The 'wilderness' area at Kilmainham is also currently being re-created. It is surrounded by a hornbeam hedge (*Carpinus betulus*) and will feature small trees along the pathways.

The terrace at Kilmainham contravenes convention in that, over the years, trees have been planted here. However, their size still allows for extensive views, and it has been decided to retain them as a record of the garden's development over the years.

In the garden, pathways lead to a central, round pond with a single-jet fountain, whose flow of water adds movement to the landscape. The walkways of the main axes are emphasized by linings of pleached lime trees, while the ancillary paths intersect four outer circular lawns. The pattern created by this layout could be said to resemble a central sun surrounded by four satellites, evoking the grandeur and rule of Louis XIV, the 'Sun King'. It is also relevant to the Ireland of the day, whose four provinces were ruled from London.

Kilmainham Hospital's five tympana on the external walls, carved in pine, depict images of war and a lion's pelt, representing the might of man, as well as peaceful images of the pastoral art of gardening.

Figurative statuary was a fashionable component of the late seventeenth and early eighteenth-century vista garden, and it has been incorporated into the ongoing re-creation project. Copies of two Liberal Arts statues have been acquired from Stowe in England, representing 'Painting' (a female figure carrying an easel) and 'Sculpture' (a female figure carrying a sculpted head). Two further statues, promised for the site, will complete a geometric square – Hercules (god of physical strength and military might) and Flora (goddess of flowers). The latter two sculptures will complete the symbolism of the post-English Civil War era, as the four works together represent the arts, war, peace and a return to nature. The figures are also appropriate and relevant today, for they reflect the arts displayed within the Museum.

Three large putti figures, which had been kept in the Hospital when it was used as a museum store, now stand on the terrace. They once embellished the base of a statue of Queen Victoria which stood at Leinster House. The classical urns along the top of the terrace's balustrades are copied from the design of those found in William and Mary's garden at Hampton Court.

The garden's walls have been rebuilt and refaced at various times over the past three centuries. A small section of the original wall remains. Today the walls are adorned with espalier trees and trellises, in imitation of the famous William III Hetloo Gardens in Holland.

At the bottom of the garden is a Garden House. It is believed to have been the work of Sir Edward Lovett Pearce, the Irish Surveyor-General, who also designed Parliament House (now the Bank of Ireland) on College Green. Pearce was appointed overseer of the Hospital in April 1731, and it is thought that he intended this building as a dining pavilion. It is currently used by the Irish Museum of Modern Art, with the assistance of the Office of Public Works, to exhibit panels describing the development, history and re-creation of the garden.

During the centuries that Kilmainham Hospital served as a home for veteran soldiers, the formal garden was also known as the Master's Garden, and a horse named 'Vonolel', which had belonged to one of the masters, was buried here. Although it is not known exactly where the horse's body lies, a commemorative headstone has been placed against one of the walls, near a newly planted mulberry tree, and serves as a constant reminder both of his life and of the history of Kilmainham. It reads: 'Beneath this stone lies Vonolel for twenty-three years the charger and faithful friend of Field Marshal Lord Roberts of Kandahar ... who died at the Royal Hospital in June 1899.'

The re-creation of Kilmainham Hospital Garden has entailed not an exact replication, but a sensitive interpretation, of classical landscape architectural features, in the context of change throughout history. The garden is a fitting companion to the Museum of Modern Art.

Detailed information on the formal gardens has been supplied courtesy of Elizabeth Morgan, Landscape Conservation Architect, at the Office of Public Works.

Opening Hours: every day during daylight hours

Buses: 79 from Aston Quay (to Heuston Station); 78A from Aston Quay (to Thomas Street)

Nearby: Kilmainham Gaol, Irish Museum of Modern Art, National War Memorial Park, Phoenix Park

---

Croppies Memorial Park

Open spaces and parks, with their greenery and trees, can offer healing and transformation to the wounds of the past. Croppies' Memorial Park is such a place. A powerful reminder of the grotesqueness of war, it commemorates the many Irish executed in 1798, when widespread rebellion against British rule was put down with grim ferocity.

Irish rebels of the 1790s were known as 'croppies' for their hair, which was closely cropped after the French Revolutionary style. The croppies, when captured, were brought to Dublin for execution. Many of these executions were carried out in the Royal Barracks (renamed Collins Barracks in the 1920s), situated on the north bank of the Liffey opposite the Guinness brewery. The barracks have been renovated and now house part of the collection of the National Museum.

At the end of the eighteenth century the Liffey filled a wider channel, and the bodies were thrown into the swampy land near the river and simply covered over.

Thus the area between the barracks and the river came to be known as 'Croppies' Acre'.

This land, now Croppies' Memorial Park, is currently managed by Dublin Corporation, and in 1984 it won a Civic Award for the excellence of its upkeep. It provides a well-placed garden for the Ashling Hotel and the bed-and-breakfast hostelries whose premises, on Parkgate Street, overlook it.

Enclosed by shrubbery and low-level hedging, its dominant feature is a central lily pond. There is also a small rose garden, while Great Maples line a pathway through the park.

Opening hours: every day during daylight hours

Nearby: Collins Museum, Phoenix Park, Kilmainham Hospital Garden

Wolfe Tone Park

A wooden sculpture stands in one corner of this park. A totem of carved faces entitled 'Universal Man', it was sculpted by Derek Williams over a two-year period, from 1991 to 1993, out of a 5000-year-old piece of bog oak from Carrow Keel, County Sligo, donated by Dan Healy. The work commemorates Theobald Wolfe Tone (1763–98), founder of republicanism in Ireland.

The sculpture was unveiled in 1993 at a ceremony attended by Tone's great, great grandson, who came over to Dublin from California for the occasion. Unfortunately, on the day, it lashed rain, and the speeches had to be made inside St Mary's Church (at that time used as a gallery) and not in the park as originally intended.

Wolfe Tone Park (better known as Jervis Street Park) was originally a graveyard attached to St Mary's Protestant church in Mary Street. In 1886 it was redesigned as a garden/park, and in the early 1960s it assumed its current layout. However, it still rings with echoes of its former life as a burial ground, for gravestones line its enclosing walls.

St Mary's Church was constructed by Thomas Burgh in 1697, under the direction of the Duke of Ormonde. The church has been associated with many famous names. Tone, who was born in adjoining Stafford Street where his father had a coach-building business, was baptized here.

Others baptized here were the Earl of Charlemont (1728), Richard Brinsley Sheridan (1751) and Sean O'Casey (1880). Among those buried in the graveyard are Lord Norbury, the Hanging Judge of 1798, while John Wesley, founder of Methodism, preached his first sermon in Ireland here in 1747, and Arthur Guinness, founder of the Guinness brewery, was married here in 1793.

In the nineteenth century, attendance waned as the north side of Dublin became less fashionable, and the final burial to be conducted here was in the 1950s. In 1986 the church was handed over to the Greek Orthodox Community for a one-year period, during which brief time it was elevated to the status of a cathedral. After this, and an ensuing period of disuse, St Mary's was converted into a gallery/workshop in 1990. In 1995 it was inhabited by Ryan's Decorating Centre, and the building is shortly to be converted again, this time into a pub.

The park, less than an acre in size, is well maintained by Dublin Corporation. A large cruciform flower-bed fills the centre, within which is a stone inscribed 'Tribute to Wolfe Tone (PATRIOT)'. With its benches, lawns, shady trees, and paths where pigeons peck at crumbs in dappled sunlight, Wolfe Tone Park is a lunchtime haven for a transient tribe of workers and shoppers. They come here for quiet reflection, a bit of gossip, or a bite to eat – a bright medley of people who enjoy the luxury of this small patch of green in the heart of the inner city, where one of Ireland's leading figures is forever remembered.

Opening hours: every day during daylight hours

Nearby: Jervis Street Shopping Centre, open 9.00–18.00 Monday–Saturday, 9.00–21.00 Thursday, 14.00–18.00 Sundays

---

Millennium Garden

The Millennium Garden, situated opposite the Olympia, one of the city's famous theatres, is itself like an audience pit, for its seating bays are set back from the street, and provide a perfect place to stop a while and perhaps reflect that 'all the world's a stage and all the men and women merely players'.

The Olympia Theatre was opened by Dan Lowry in 1879. It was the city's first regular music hall, known as The Star of Erin. At that time its main entrance was in Crampton Court, around the corner, and it was not until after the theatre's reconstruction in 1897 that the main door was moved to Dame Street. The theatre was then re-named the Empire Theatre of Varieties, and its repertoire was expanded from musical variety to include plays, revues and pantomimes. There used to be two nightly per-formances at the theatre. The queue for the circle formed around Crampton Court, and those who hadn't gained entrance to the first show were entertained by street singers, mouth organists, jugglers and dulcimer players.

The Millennium Garden was constructed in 1988 to mark the thousand-year anniversary of the founding of the city of Dublin. It provides a welcome splash of colour to Dame Street's townscape, and with Dublin Castle behind it, City Hall next to it and the Olympia Theatre opposite, the Garden occupies an historically interesting site. Here once stood a row of houses, among which was

Dr Thomas Barnardo's birthplace (1845). John Michaelis Barnardo, Thomas's father, of exiled Spanish Protestant descent, had emigrated to Ireland from Germany, and he ran a wholesale furrier business from No. 4 Dame Street. Thomas moved to London in 1866 to study medicine, and it was there he became involved in what was to be his outstanding life-long work with homeless children, as a result of which Barnardo's Homes came into being.

The Garden is accessed by steps, as well as a ramp. It has circular lawns, with trees and shrubbery behind, and a linear flower-bed at the front, adjacent to the pavement. A pond, with ten fountain heads, stands in one corner, decorated by robust statues – female figures which represent the crafts of wood, metal and stone. These used to reside at the Exhibition Palace in Earlsfort Terrace, which is now the National Concert Hall.

Opening hours: this park, opening directly onto the street, never closes

Nearby: Olympia Theatre, Dublin Castle, Dubh Linn Garden, Christchurch Cathedral, Trinity College

---

Dubh Linn Garden

Built on a seventy-metre square plot of land, Dubh Linn Garden's circular, central lawn doubles as a helicopter pad! Based on the 'parterre' garden, which features much ornamentation and is looked down upon from a height, its lawn displays formal and traditional Celtic patterning, using a serpent motif derived from the Book of Kells. Similar decoration is evident in the garden's wrought-iron gates and railings, and ties in, too, with the zoomorphic representations of Oriental art in the adjoining Chester Beatty Gallery.

Vantage points from which to view the garden are created through a raised pathway outside the Coach House, and by a ramp leading across a tower and over a bridge to Dublin Castle's State Apartments, which serves as a ceremonial route for visting dignitaries. The serpents' bodies, pavement snaking through grass, are studded with lights to represent eyes. By night, when these are illuminated for use as landing guides, they sparkle like the multi-faceted jewels encrusted on a Celtic sword.

This public garden cum helipad, formally a derelict patch of grass, was created in six months, from June to December 1994, in anticipation of the arrival by helicopter of dignitaries visiting Dublin Castle during the Irish Presidency of the European Union in 1995.

The central lawn measures fifty square metres in diameter, and has two landing pads – one space serves as a decoy to confuse would-be assassins. It has a base of sand, for landing a helicopter requires a hard and compacted surface. This land had been used as a temporary burial ground for the officers and soldiers shot dead during the 1916 Rising, prior to their ceremonial reinterment. During the Second World War it was occupied by air-raid shelters, and, following that, for a short time it was a football pitch.

In the Bronze Age, the area had been a sheltered harbour, known as Dubh Linn (Black Pool), which formed where the River Poddle, now culverted underground, joins the Liffey. The harbour was used as the staging post for exports and imports to Dubh Linn's ecclesiastical settlement immediately south of the present-day Castle.

Round about the garden a multitude of disparate buildings dot the horizon. However, the enveloping, busy jigsaw of architecture does not detract from the garden's integrity, for its central lawn is enclosed within a low circular wall, which unifies the elements within it, and it is decorated with a ring of blue lavender which further reinforces its shape. The colour also reflects the granite and Killaloe slate with which the lawn's surrounding path is made, as well as the granite face of some of the surrounding buildings, while the emphatic bluish tinge of plants throughout – such as rosemary, curry plants and eucalyptus – further complements the colour scheme.

Pathways interlink the four small corner gardens, each

of which has an individual character and contains a commissioned piece of artwork. There's a square black pool, a Celtic snake, a mosaic, and a rain bowl. Every installation features water. All reflect elements of the colour, shape or decoration found in the central garden, and all display historical features relating to the area.

Dublin Castle, constructed in the thirteenth century on the orders of King John, by architect Meiler Fitzhenry, had by the mid-sixteenth century fallen into disrepair. Its renovation was carried out between 1566 and 1570, under the auspices of the then Lord Lieutenant, Sir Henry Sidney,

who was responsible for building the new viceregal residence where, today, the State Apartments stand.

Overlooking the garden, the Bermingham Tower formed the main cell and dungeon section of the Castle. It is named after Sir William de Bermingham, who was imprisoned and hanged for treason there in 1331. It had to be rebuilt in 1777, following structural damage caused by an explosion in the nearby armoury.

Adjoining this tower, in the same block, are the State Apartments; an octagonal tower (built on the site of an original D-shaped tower which had been destroyed by fire in 1684); the Chapel Royal; and the Record Tower. The chapel was designed by Francis Johnston in 1807, and was opened on Christmas Day 1814. It has since been renamed the Church of the Most Holy Trinity.

The Record Tower, once a top-security prison, was made famous through Red Hugh O'Donnell, the Donegal chieftain's son, who was an Irish patriot and a rebel against the Crown. Having already escaped in 1591 from imprisonment in the Gate Tower, he was recaptured in 1592 and imprisoned in the stronghold of the Record Tower. However, in the same year he escaped again and returned to Donegal, where he joined with his neighbour Hugh O'Neill to fight for the Irish cause, in what is known as 'The Nine Year War'. The rebels were eventually routed in Co. Cork in 1601. O'Donnell was forced to flee to Spain, and he died in 1602 at Simancas and was buried with full state honours at the monastery of San Francisco in Valladolid, home of the Spanish King's court.

The Coach House borders the garden's southern side. Its castellated frontage had been erected to give Queen Victoria a regal view from the State Apartments, where she stayed during her visit to Ireland in 1849. Subsequently, it was used as a scaffolding store by the Office of Public Works. It has now been converted into a conference centre, and is often used by the press during political talks.

Other buildings within the immediate vicinity include the Garda barracks, Garda Carriage Office, and the Chester Beatty Library and Gallery of Oriental Art. In their midst, Dubh Linn Garden offers a new and unique piece of landscape architecture.

Opening hours: every day during daylight hours

Nearby: Christchurch Cathedral, St Patrick's Cathedral

Peace Park

This park is situated opposite Christchurch Cathedral in a small and somewhat bleak corner next to Jury's Hotel at the top of Lord Edward Street. It occupies an area formerly known as the Tholsel, a meeting place for the City Council and other bodies, such as merchants, who used the building as an exchange in the fourteenth century. It was here that the City Recorder's Courts held their sessions, and alleged criminals received punishments, one such being a whipping from the Tholsel as far as College Green. A whipping post and pillory used to stand in front of the Tholsel, but these were removed before the 1790s, while the two statues over its entrance, and the city stocks, are now on display in Christchurch crypt.

The park is designed as a circular, sunken garden, with a central pond and fountain, surrounded by seating bays and rose borders. It also has a built-up area of heathers, conifers and Star-of-Bethlehem.

A plaque on a side wall of this park recalls the Peace Train of 30 October 1995. It explains how Tony Whelan, a Dublin bricklayer, with the support of the Bricklayers and Allied Trades Union, dedicated one new brick to each of the twenty-six District Councils of Northern Ireland, to symbolize the rebuilding necessary after bomb explosions. Also mentioned is the fact that at Portadown Railway Station, the Mayor, Councillor Joy Savage, presented a brick recovered from a bombed site in Craigavon to Tomás MacGiolla, Lord Mayor of Dublin. Recorded, too, is the fact that eight hundred people travelled on the Peace Train.

Opening hours: every day during daylight hours

Nearby: Christchurch Cathedral, Mother Redcap's Market, Dublin Castle

St Catherine's Park

One of the oldest parks in Dublin lurks at the back of the Protestant Church of St Catherine in Thomas Street, like a coy child hiding behind the skirts of its mother. A bronze seat by Tom Flavin, titled 'Adult and Child Seat' (1988), stands like a giant seaside rock in one corner of the park, while plain benches line the paths made from old granite setts and limestone dust.

The park was once a graveyard serving the church, and headstones lined up against an enclosing wall, old, worn and barely decipherable, hark back to the past. Other headstones stand inside a ring of trees at the centre. A plaque set inside the gate reads, 'The Rt Hon The Lord Mayor of Dublin, Alderman Jim Tunney TD, officially opened this park to the public on June 20th 1986.'

The Church of St Catherine is named after the chapel belonging to St Thomas Abbey, which stood on the site before the Reformation. Designed by John Smyth and built between 1760 and 1769, it is emblematic of the ever mutable face of the city, constantly under threat of further change. For, since 1966, St Catherine's has not been used as a church. Instead, under the custodianship of Dublin Corporation, recitals and concerts have been held here, and now, currently redundant and boarded up, it is subject to Planning Application with Dublin Corporation for change of use. One wonders will it be a commercial, artistic or cultural function that brings St Catherine's into the twenty-first century?

At the front of the church, a plaque and monument commemorate the life of Robert Emmet, who, having led a band of rebels to kill Lord Kilwarden and his nephew, was then himself executed here in September 1803.

Perhaps it is appropriate that among the trees that grow in the park are two species reputed to have healing as well as protective qualities – the ash and the rowan. According to legend, a crippled or diseased child would be cured if passed through the cleft of an ash, while the rowan was considered to be a charm against witches.

Opening hours: every day during daylight hours

Nearby: Guinness Hop Store

St Audoen's Park

Stepping into St Audoen's Park is like stepping back in time. Situated on high ground, behind Dublin's ancient and castellated city walls, and screened from its immediate environment by a shrubbery border, it retains a medieval atmosphere.

The park is the ideal focal point from which to explore medieval Dublin, for it is located in one of the oldest parts of the city. It can be found next to St Audoen's Church, which was built in 1190 following the Norman conquest of Ireland in 1170. The church, dedicated to the Norman Saint 'Ouen', replaced a Celtic chapel that had stood on the same site, consecrated to Colmcille (who died in 597).

Once a graveyard annexe to St Audoen's Church, the park was developed in 1981 by Dublin Corporation, and was officially opened to the public in 1982, winning in the process a Civic Award. Approximately one acre in size, it is now laid to lawn with pathways and attractive seating bays constructed from old granite setts.

Along one walkway, two memorial plaques recall the lives of notable Irishmen born in the vicinity. The first, a dedication to Charles A. Callis (1865–1947), a latter-day saint, commemorates the 150th anniversary of the Church of Jesus Christ of Latter Day Saints (the Mormons) in Britain and Ireland in 1987. The second is a dedication to James Napper Tandy (1740–1803), secretary of the Dublin Society of United Irishmen.

Like most mediaeval cities, Dublin had been enclosed by stone walls, intersected at intervals with gates and towers. Dublin's city walls date back to 1170. They reached inland, in a ring from Merchants' Quay and Wood Quay to beyond Christchurch Cathedral.

St Audoen's stands inside what had been the inner wall (the second line of defence) in the highest part of old Dublin lands. A section of the original wall still exists in Cook Street, and forms a boundary to the church and park. It adjoins St Audoen's Gate (1240), the last remaining of Dublin's thirty-two gates, which can be reached via the famous 'Forty Steps' leading from the park.

In 1448 the area within the City Walls where St Audoen's is situated was designated 'The Pale' (from the Latin 'Palus', meaning 'stake' and, by derivation, 'defensive enclosure'). It became the administrative headquarters of the city. Following the Reformation, St Audoen's Parish was an enclave of prosperous Protestant merchants. In Victorian times, however, the Protestant population of the area dwindled from 800 in 1831, to 274 in 1881, and nowadays, although St Audoen's Church is still used for services, these are not on a grand scale as before, but are held in a small chapel. The building, which still retains some of its original Norman fabric, underwent extensive restoration in 1826, and at various times subsequently. Further major restoration is in progress.

A feature of interest, firmly fixed to the wall inside its porch, is 'The Lucky Stone' – an early Christian head-stone, having associations with a ghostly priest, and reputed to have occult powers. The stone had previously stood in a corner of St Audoen's tower, where it could be touched by passers-by. However, having been stolen in

1826, and then recovered after many adventures, it was removed to its present, more secure position.

Opening hours: every day during daylight hours

Nearby: Christchurch Cathedral, Mother Redcap's Market

St Patrick's Park

This park suggests an open-air ballroom, with the central fountain, spilling water on a summer's day and catching rainbows in the sun, a giant chandelier. Meanwhile, looking on, St Patrick's Cathedral, massive and handsome, is like an ever-watchful matriarchal figure standing in the wings.

However, such a ballroom scene could not have been more remote at the turn of the century when the park was a piece of waste land, used as a right of way to and from the run-down tenement buildings surrounding it.

A veritable Cinderella, the area was converted into a respectable park between 1903 and 1905 through the intervention of the munificent Guinness family. Since then it has been further restored through the generosity of Jameson's Irish Whiskies and the publicans of Dublin. Now under Dublin Corporation's management, it offers a stately open space in one of the oldest parts of the city.

Although the park is devoid of trees along the inner pathways, limes and planes line the Bull Alley and St

Patrick Street boundaries, and neat flower-beds display seasonal colour, interposed with areas of shrubbery and two red-flowered Cotoneasters.

The massive stone features in the park – a large central pond and fountain and another acorn motif fountain – seem larger than life, while Vivienne Roche's bronze sculpture 'Liberty Bell' appropriately reflects the ecclesiastical connection. This connection is reflected back, in that Jonathan Swift was Dean of the Cathedral; and it seems fitting, therefore, that a 'Literary Parade' was installed in the park in 1988 to honour some of Ireland's distinguished writers.

Opening hours: every day during daylight hours

Nearby: St Patrick's Cathedral, Christchurch Cathedral, Francis St antique shops

---

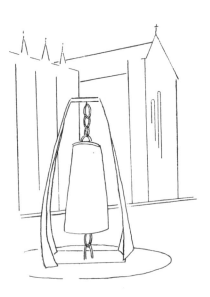

St Kevin's Park

St Kevin's Park can be found between Camden Row and Liberty Lane, next to Kevin Street Technical College, where it nestles behind high stone retaining walls. It has about it something of an old walled cottage garden, and on a summer's day the sun dapples the scene as in a Mary Swanzy painting.

Converted to a park by Dublin Corporation in 1962, it had formerly been a graveyard to St Kevin's Church, built in 1226, which, though now a ruin, still stands in the centre of the park and is an impenetrable shell. Its entrance and windows are safely sealed off by bars, and its walls are protected by an impassable covering of ivy.

Located within earshot of the bells of St Patrick's Cathedral, the park is pleasant as a place to sit and relax, but it is also a shrine to some of the renowned figures from Ireland's past. Headstones commemorate Jasper Joly, who sheltered Lord Edward Fitzgerald, and John Keogh, the United Irishman.

Another stone commemorates Dermot O'Hurley (b.

1530), Archbishop of Cashel, who was executed in 1584, for alleged treason. He is said to be buried inside the church, in a 'secret' grave. His martyrdom inspired frequent pilgrimages to the site.

St Kevin's Park is currently well tended, with lawns, pathways, flowerbeds, and, among other trees, a cherry and a golden yew.

Opening hours: every day during daylight hours

Nearby: St Patrick's Cathedral, St Stephen's Green, Iveagh Gardens

Garden of
Remembrance

We sent our vision aswim like a swan on a river:
The vision became a reality, Winter became Summer
Bondage became freedom ...
O generations of freedom remember us,
the generation of the vision.
    —Liam MacUistin, 'We Saw a Vision'

The Garden of Remembrance in Parnell Square com-
memorates those who gave their lives for the cause of
Irish freedom. Its gestation was slow. The concept of a
memorial garden was first suggested in 1935 by the
Dublin Brigade Council of the old IRA. In 1946 Daithi P.
Hanly won a competition for its design. Work on the
Garden started in 1961, and it was officially opened on
Easter Monday 1966, the Golden Anniversary of the
Easter Rising, by President Eamon de Valera.

The Garden occupies the site of the former Vauxhall Gardens, which were attached to the Rotunda Hospital. (The Rotunda was built by architect Richard Johnston between 1750 and 1757, at the bequest of a Dr Bartholomew Mosse. It is the oldest maternity hospital in the world.)

At the time of the hospital's construction, this part of Dublin was particularly fashionable, and the Vauxhall Gardens, together with their adjoining Assembly Rooms,

had an admission fee, which it was thought the local residents could easily afford, the purpose of which was to offset the cost of building the hospital. (The Assembly Rooms were also built by Richard Johnston, between 1784 and 1786, and in 1929 they were taken over by Micheál MacLiammóir and Hilton Edwards to house the Gate Theatre, founded in 1928.)

It was in the Vauxhall Gardens that, in 1915, Óglaigh na hÉireann (the Irish Volunteers) were formed. It was here, too, that after the Irish surrender on the Saturday of Easter Week, 1916, rebel prisoners were stockaded overnight, in the open.

The Garden of Remembrance is now maintained by Dúchas. Its dominant feature is Oisín Kelly's twenty-five-foot high, eight-ton bronze sculpture, cast in the Marinelli Foundry in Florence, entitled 'The Children of Lir', dated 1971. The piece was inspired by the Irish mythological tale of the same name telling of children transmuted into swans for 900 years by their wicked stepmother.

At the centre of the Garden is a long cruciform pool, whose mosaic lining depicts spears dating back to the Heroic Age, 300 BC to 300 AD. They are shown broken, an invocation of the Celtic custom of hurling weapons into lakes and rivers once battle was over.

Further features include decorative railings, which enclose the lawns of the park. Again, the images are traditional. They derive from artefacts in the National Museum – Brian Boru's harp, the Loughnashade Trumpet (100 BC) and the Ballinderry Sword (200 BC), which points downwards, indicating peace.

Across the street from the Garden's north side the National Ballroom can be found. The ballroom was purchased by Dublin Corporation in 1995, and there are plans for it to be converted into a complex housing a 200-seat theatre, with a mezzanine level to be used as exhibition space. The Irish Writers' Museum and the Hugh Lane Municipal Gallery of Modern Art are also on the north side of the Garden.

The Municipal Gallery occupies Charlemont House, which was built between 1762 and 1766 by William Chambers, architect for Lord Charlemont. Its frontage was so magnificently ornate that, in the late eighteenth century, it earned this side of Parnell Square the nickname 'Palace Row'.

The Abbey Presbyterian Church, or 'Findlater's Church', as it is more commonly known, is located on the corner of the square and Frederick Street North. Its construction was made possible through the financial assistance of Alexander Findlater, a Scots brewer and grocer prominent in business in Dublin, who donated the £14,000 required for building to go ahead. It is neo-gothic in style and its spire is one hundred and eighty feet high.

Opening hours:
January–February 11.00–16.00
March–April 11.00–19.00
May–September 9.30–20.00
October 11.00–19.00
November–December 11.00–16.00
Christmas Day 11.00–13.00
(Opening times are subject to change.)

Nearby: Hugh Lane Municipal Gallery of Modern Art, Gate Theatre, James Joyce Centre

---

Mountjoy Square Park

An extraordinary thing happened in Mountjoy Square in 1983. One afternoon, the top storey of No. 64, next to Discount Electric, collapsed into the street below, crushing a parked car under a ton of bricks and masonry. No one was hurt, although people had walked past the building within seconds of the event. A cocker spaniel, left under the seat of the car, survived, and was freed by firemen using cutting equipment. The building had been empty for some time and its structure had become unstable. Fortunately, it has now been safely restored and is ready again for habitation.

When Mountjoy Square was built, between 1792 and 1818, it was hailed as one of the city's finest, being symmetrical, with a total of sixty-eight houses. It was known as Gardiner Square in the planning stages, after Luke Gardiner, Lord Mountjoy, who was responsible for its construction, and it only became known as Mountjoy Square after building had started.

The park was enclosed in 1801. Initially, the intention

was to build a church at its centre. However, that idea was abandoned in favour of a cheaper solution, which was to plant an ash tree, with a circular path around it, in the middle of the land.

At the beginning of the nineteenth century the square housed the cream of society, among them Archbishop Hawkesley at No. 1, and Alderman John Campbell, twice mayor of the city, at No. 27. There was also a Crown Solicitor, Piers Geale, at No. 65, who became well known because he encouraged titled men to court his daughter, a fact which resulted in his residence being known as 'The House of Lords'.

By 1805 four gates had been placed in the railings of the square and one hundred keys were issued among residents for their private use. In 1832 the grounds were

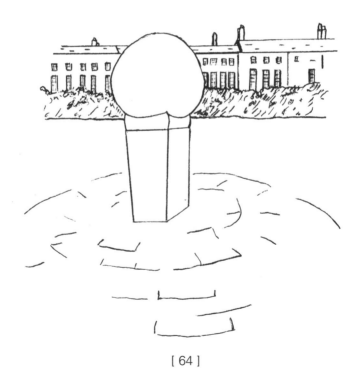

opened up to the inhabitants of the adjoining roads, and by 1836 the general public were granted access. However, there was a prohibition on smoking.

Records show that bands played in the park from 1863, a croquet lawn was established in 1866, and tennis courts were set up in 1881 (although without the same prestige as those of Fitzwilliam Square). In 1894 the square's commissioners were successful in preventing the square from being used as a thoroughfare for transporting cattle from the market to the docks.

Over the course of the nineteenth century Dublin's south side had become the place to live. Mountjoy Square witnessed an exodus, and the area around it began to decline in prestige as single-family houses became tenements. Whereas in 1848 thirty-four lawyers and four doctors lived in the Square, by 1928 there was only one lawyer and one doctor. The working-class playwright Sean O'Casey lived at No. 35 for five months in 1920 and it is thought that 'Hillroy Square' in his play *The Shadow of a Gunman* was inspired by his sojourn there.

In a bid to save the Square from dereliction in the 1960s, John Molloy of the Georgian Society and Desmond Guinness bought Nos 47 and 50 respectively. Both these owners have long since moved, but the restoration of the square has continued. The gracious façades of the Square's houses have been conserved, but, like most of Dublin's other Georgian squares, the function of the various premises has changed from family dwellings to office premises or small apartments. The Dublin Institute of Technology School of Marketing and Design occupies Nos 40–45 on the south-east side.

Meanwhile, it was back in 1938 that Dublin Corporation took over the maintenance of the park, converting it into a playground in 1947. Currently, the park is roughly divided into two. On one side there is a play area, a games pitch and a nursery. On the other side there are well-tended gardens, whose lawns are lined with pathways and seating areas. There is also an attractive rose garden which is centred around a sundial and is surrounded by a shrubbery border.

Opening hours: every day during daylight hours

Nearby: James Joyce Centre

Blessington Street Basin

Above the outside enclosing walls of this park, terraced houses peep like spectators in the gods. A cobbled path leads to gates at east and west, around a reservoir, with a central island bird sanctuary. A heron comes out from the undergrowth periodically to take a bow. Bees suck pollen inside purple fuchsia bells, while mallards and moorhens dip and dive and play.

Entering the park from the right, two men run past in jogging shorts. From the left, two women pass, carrying shopping, and wheeling a child in a pushchair. A man and woman, tourists, it seems, stroll slowly, arm in arm, and stop to read a plaque on the wall which describes the sculptures indented in the wall, made by local students. An ol' fella enters from the right and stops, leaning over the iron railings, to look at the water.

The Black Church's bell peals out across the air and blends with a balmy fragrance of lavender and roses. The colours of fuchsias, snapdragons and curry plants reach up in sweet embrace, while the roar and rumble of traffic outside tells of a different reality.

The Basin is tucked away at the end of Blessington Street and, otherwise known as 'The Secret Garden', it provides a sanctuary for local residents and visitors alike. It dates back to 1809, and water was first supplied to it via the Royal Canal, from Lough Owel, north of Mullingar.

Its main claim to fame is that, from the 1860s until the 1970s, water from it was used to supply the Jameson's and Power's whiskey distilleries for both cooling and malting. This only ceased when distillation moved to Midleton, Co. Cork.

Extensive refurbishment was completed on the Basin in 1994. Among the enhancements are 1200 square metres of trees, shrubs, herbaceous and annual bedding plants, cobbled seating bays, wrought-iron seats, and ornamental lampposts. Its modernization blends well

with the surrounding Georgian and Victorian houses, and the park, like a glorious theatre, is imbued with a sense of timelessness.

Opening hours: every day during daylight hours

Nearby: King's Inns

King's Inns Park

King's Inns Park enhances the front of King's Inns, which is one of three architectural masterpieces in Dublin by James Gandon – the other two being the Custom House (1781) and the Four Courts (1786).

King's Inns (built between 1800 and 1817) was originally intended as part of a larger scheme, to include a further crescent-shaped building, along Constitution Hill and facing the Inns across a central, collegiate-style quad. The Inns was to house the Law Library and the dining hall, while the additional building was intended as barristers' chambers. However, due to financial difficulties and Gandon's early retirement from the project in 1808, the second building was never built. The fact that such a building was planned helps to explain the bizarre physical position of King's Inns, facing west across Constitution Hill, and with its back at an angle across Henrietta Street.

King's Inns straddles what had been two separately owned parcels of land. On the right was the Plover Field,

owned by Luke Gardiner, Lord Mountjoy, while on the left was the Primate's Lawn, which was the property of the Dean and Chapter of Christchurch. The two pieces of land were linked by a pathway, which Gandon incorporated as a connecting courtyard through the Inns from Henrietta Street to Constitution Hill.

Once Gandon had retired, Francis Johnston took over the work on King's Inns. He completed the Dining Hall and converted the partially built library into a Registry of Deeds, which function it still fulfils today, occupying two thirds of the building. The remaining one third of the premises is all that is now owned by Dublin's legal body, and it is here that legal courses and lectures are held, while Barristers' Chambers can be found in Church Street, near the Four Courts.

Four sculptures (by the nineteenth-century sculptor Edward Smyth) embellish the Inns' two main entrance doors. On either side of the Dining Hall are Ceres (Goddess of Plenty) and a Bacchante (a follower of Bacchus, God of Wine) holding a goblet.

The male figures at the entrance to the Registry of Deeds are 'Law', holding a book and quill, and 'Security', holding a key and scroll. Immediately opposite the building, in the grounds of the park, is a further sculptured female figure. Her symbolic significance is not known, but she was transferred to the King's Inns from the Four Courts in 1880. She faces inwards, and is known locally as 'Henrietta'.

The term 'Inns of Court' derives from the custom of student barristers sharing common lodgings as part of their social training. (It was thought that the best way to inculcate and maintain professional and gentlemanly conduct would be through proximity to one's fellow legal aspirants.) Formal dinners were also a form of training, when students were expected to learn through listening to their elders' dinner-time conversation.

'Inns' have been recorded in Ireland since the reign of King Edward I. The first, in 1300, was Collett's Inns, situated near the present-day Exchequer Street. In 1384 they were relocated to where City Hall now stands, at which point they became known as Preston's Inns. Later, in 1541, following the dissolution of the monasteries, King Henry VIII presented the Dominican Friary of St Saviour at Inns Quay to the Irish legal body. At this point they gained the denomination 'King's' as a mark of gratitude to the Crown. Towards the end of the eighteenth century the latter premises had become derelict, and the site was appropriated for the building of the Four Courts. A new location for the Inns was needed, and it was then that the Henrietta Street site was acquired. The Inns have remained there ever since.

A new Law Library was established at the top of Henrietta Street in 1827. Two and a half centuries later, in the mid 1970s, it became the butt of a scandal, because of the sale by the Irish legal body of rare and valuable books at Sotheby's in London. The sale was prompted by a need to raise money for the maintenance and repair of the Inns. However, historians and librarians throughout Ireland objected to the sale on the grounds of the rarity and cultural importance of the books.

An Taisce (the Irish National Trust) interceded on behalf of Trinity College, the National Library and Maynooth College with the result that several volumes were withdrawn from sale, and a number of works were bought back. One was 'A Christian Instruction Composed Long Ago' by Cardinal Richelieu, printed in Paris in 1662, of which only one other copy is known to exist, at Yale University.

Through the scandal, the legal body had drawn attention to its financial difficulties, and in 1986 a grant of £600,000 was provided through government funding under the Suitors Bill to carry out major restoration work on the Inns. Happily, part of this funding was spent on repairing the enclosing wall of the park along Constitution Hill.

Currently the park is maintained by Dublin Corporation. It is open to the public daily and offers a pleasant, enclosed area of lawn, dotted with trees and seating bays. Next to the Constitution Hill Gate stands a London plane tree. It is approximately one hundred years old, and sprawls over a cast-iron bench.

The story goes that, as the tree matured, its girth expanded and gradually merged into the bench. Of course, had Gandon's original plan to build along the Constitution Hill side of the land come to fruition, the bench would not have existed at all! As it is, bench and tree, which together are something of a quaint curiosity, add character, as well as a note of eccentricity, to an already extraordinary building.

Opening hours: every day during daylight hours

Nearby: Blessington Street Basin

National Botanic Gardens

All year at the National Botanic Gardens in Glasnevin there is activity and all year there is colour. Wheelbarrows along paths and verges signify pruning, planting and growth. In winter heathers carpet the ground, rhododendron flowers startle the bleakness, pink 'Disco Dancer' and 'Samouri' roses bloom. In summer the herbaceous border displays the rich reds, oranges, yellows and purples of bright flowers such as dahlias, marigolds and poppies.

Founded by the Dublin Society in 1795 on a site of sixteen Irish acres, the Gardens now cover some fifty statute acres. They contain a diversity of trees and herbaceous plants, sculptures and architecture (including the restored Richard Turner curvilinear range of glasshouses), and an attractive landscape featuring the Tolka River, the mill race and undulating grounds. Their appeal is to botanist, horticulturist and general public alike.

My favourite section is the 'Burren Garden', which can be found within the conservation area beyond the new library by the vegetable garden. The garden replicates the phenomenal landscape of north-west County Clare. Large fissured wedges of grey limestone are intersected by delicate flowers whose names, like figwort, pyramidal bugle or mouse-ear hawkweed, have a magical ring. Their filigreed appearance is somehow incongruous against the hard rock.

For the first-time visitor to the Gardens, a tour might include the curvilinear glasshouses and the water-house complex, a walk along the herbaceous border to the pond, a stroll along the Tolka River to the rose garden

and a return to the palm house. Highlights to watch out for might include the tender vireya rhododendron in the curvilinear range, the Killarney fern (a protected species) in the fern house, the stone plants from South Africa in the cactus house and the banana plant in the palm house. Then there's the pampas grass in the herbaceous border, which was introduced into cultivation in Ireland from Argentina, and near the pond there's a giant redwood tree (native of the Sierra Nevada, USA). Outside the palm house, a collection of native and exotic strawberry trees can be found.

Botanic gardens are based on the 'physic gardens' originally attached to universities, and used for medical educational purposes. The first physic garden was recorded at the University of Pisa in 1543. Today, the objectives of the Gardens at Glasnevin are conservation, recreation, demonstration, education and research, and various lectures and courses are held here.

Good relationships are maintained with other Irish gardens through an exchange of seeds and plants. Glasnevin currently boasts over twenty thousand different indoor and outdoor species and cultivated varieties of plant from habitats as diverse as tundra, rainforest, desert and bog. Orchids from Belize in Central America are among the more recent acquisitions.

In 1995 the Gardens celebrated their bicentenary, and an oakwood sculpture by Gerard Cox, entitled 'Craobh', was presented by Sean Tinney, President of the Royal Dublin Society. It can be seen near the shattered Cedar of Lebanon, west of the double herbaceous borders.

The restoration of Richard Turner's curvilinear range of glasshouses also took place in 1995. A special paint, named 'Turner White', was developed to cover the ironwork and successfully achieved a match with the original colour. The restoration project, costing some £3.5 million to complete, won the Office of Public Works a Europa Nostra gold medal in 1997 for its excellence and faithfulness to the original.

Today the Gardens are maintained by Dúchas. Only a twenty-minute bus ride from Dublin city centre, they constitute, in the words of their first Director, Dr Walter Wade, Dublin's 'brightest jewel'.

Guided tours by prior arrangement. Tel. (01) 8377596, (01) 8374388; fax (01) 8360080

Opening hours:
March–October
Monday–Saturday 09.00–18.00; Sunday 11.00–18.00

November–February
Monday–Saturday 10.00–16.30; Sunday 11.00–16.30

GLASS HOUSES:
March–October
Monday–Wednesday & Friday 9.00–17.15
Thursday 9.00–15.15; Sunday 14.00–17.45

November–February
Monday–Saturday 10.00–16.15
Thursday 10.00–15.15; Sunday 14.00–16.15

Glass Houses are closed Monday to Friday, 12.45–14.00 and Saturday 12.15–14.00 all year round.

ALPINE HOUSES:
All year Monday–Friday 10.45–12.15, 14.15–15.15; Sunday 14.00–17.45; closed Saturdays; public holidays 9.00–12.45, 14.00–17.45

Buses: 19, 19A, 13 from O'Connell Street; 134 from Middle Abbey Street.

Pearse Square

The street names in Victorian Dublin often reflected English rule, and this square is no exception, for its former name was 'Queen's Square'.

Situated in the centre of a residential square that opens north from Pearse Street, this gated park has only recently been landscaped. Dublin Corporation began work on it in 1996, and it was opened in the summer of 1998. Its box hedging, shrubs, and seating bays now add to the aesthetic value of the area.

In the 1930s the park had a bandstand, and music was played on Sundays. However, changing fortunes over ensuing years meant that houses became tenements; the square's inhabitants moved out of the city, and the park fell into neglect.

The park was redesigned, but in a functional rather than aesthetic way, to suit the needs of the square's local inhabitants. For instance, part of the area was tarmacadamed, to serve as a playground. Also, a football pitch was established, and a Community Centre building was erected, which was used as a venue for leisure activities every weekend.

Pearse Square is only a ten-minute walk from the centre of town, and, newly established, neat and pretty, it has become a noticeable landmark on the way to Ringsend.

Opening hours: every day during daylight hours

Nearby: Trinity College. St Andrew's Hall Health Food Mart, opposite the square, is open Saturday mornings from 10.30.

Merrion Square Park

Summer in Merrion Square Park sees the flower garden ablaze with glorious clashing swirls of colour – reds, oranges, purples, pinks. There are round, oval and rectangular beds of geraniums, marigolds and petunias, some centred about small conical evergreen trees, like fondant fancies topped with luscious decoration.

For autumn and winter, brightness and interest are provided by the heather garden. In curved beds, the heathers spread around miniature conifers and natural tree-bark sculptures which peer from the earth, like creatures from another planet.

The most significant season for Merrion Square Park, however, is spring. The park's keepers boast that its collection of one hundred and fifty thousand spring bulbs is unsurpassed in the world – daffodils, tulips, crocuses, snowdrops, grape hyacinths, wallflowers, crown imperials, pansies and lilies perfume the air with heady fragrance.

Part of the magic of the park derives from the manmade busts, plaques and sculptures that gaze out, unexpected, from flower beds and bushes. Among the busts are Michael Collins (1880–1922); Henry Grattan (1746–1820); Bernardo O'Higgins (1778–1842, 'Liberator of Chile'); and 'Conscience Head' by Elizabeth Frink, erected in 1983 to remind people that Nelson Mandela was still incarcerated. A stone commemorating Holles Street Hospital is inscribed with a poem, 'Tree of Life', by Eavan Boland, dedicated to the still-born child.

The newest sculptural work in the park is a monument to Oscar Wilde by Danny Osborne. In keeping with Wilde's flamboyant style Osborne used colourful stone. Oscar's head and hands are solid porcelain, his shoes black Indian granite, his shoelaces bronze, and his trousers blue pearl granite from Norway. Reclining on a thirty-five-ton block of quartz from Wicklow, he looks across the road to No. 1 Merrion Square, his home from 1855 to 1878 (now The American College).

Opposite him, two small symbolic bronze figures face inwards. Dionysius, God of drama, wine and festivals, symbolizes art, maleness and the turning of sexual convention on its head. Constance, Oscar's wife, six and a half months pregnant, symbolizes the female, and life.

The bronzes stand on a rectangular plinth into which are etched a total of forty-eight quotations from Wilde's writings, selected by leading figures in their own handwriting and filled with coloured cement to look like ink.

Until the 1930s Merrion Square Park was the property of the Earls of Pembroke and was leased to residents of the Square for their private use. In the 1930s it was taken over by the Catholic Archdiocese of Dublin, and, under the auspices of Archbishop Byrne, a cathedral was planned for the site, at which time, and in conjunction with the building concept, the Central Catholic Library moved from Hawkins Street to 74 Merrion Square, where it remains to this day. Lack of funding meant that plans for the cathedral were put in abeyance and, perhaps providentially, it never did materialize. Not only would the cost of building have been prohibitive, but later, in the 1960s, the new conservation laws would have made the project difficult.

The park was considered later in the 1930s as a potential site for the National War Memorial Garden. Once again, however, costs for this project would have proved prohibitive. The plan was dropped and Islandbridge was selected as the more suitable site.

In 1974 the Catholic Archdiocese, headed by Archbishop Ryan, decided to lease the park to Dublin Corporation for public use, and to honour the Archbishop for his magnanimity it was officially renamed 'Archbishop Ryan Park'. This was probably the most suitable outcome, for with its many and diverse artistic and horticultural features in the centre of Dublin the park can now be enjoyed by all.

In style, it harks back to the Victorian era. Limestone cobbled setts are used for the garden's verges and traditional box-hedging lines the lawns. Ninety per cent evergreen and ten per cent deciduous trees, including some massive planes, ensure greenery throughout the year, while the emphasis on year-round bedding adheres to the Victorian high-maintenance form of gardening. The park covers twelve and three quarters acres, and is one of the best kept in Europe. Its neat flower garden, miniature arboretum, heather garden and open lawns are integrated by clumps of trees and tree-arched pathways. Surrounded by a fourteen-foot-thick border of shrubs within enclosing railings, the park achieves a sense of retreat from the outside world.

Opening hours: every day during daylight hours

Nearby: Oscar Wilde's former home at No.1 Merrion Square, National Gallery, Natural History Museum, National Museum, Government Buildings, Kildare Street

Fitzwilliam Square Park

The finely proportioned houses around this park, many with first-floor balconies decorated by bright window-boxes, typify Georgian splendour, and their vivid display of doors – blues, reds, yellows, and greens – presents a colourful face to the world.

Named after the 6th Lord Fitzwilliam of Merrion, one of the principal developers of the city, Fitzwilliam Square is situated at the core of a well-preserved part of Georgian Dublin. It was built in 1825, following the construction of Fitzwilliam Street (1780) and Fitzwilliam Place (1800). Initially, an appeal was launched against building the south side of the square (the last to be developed) on the grounds that it would obstruct the view of the Dublin mountains enjoyed by the other three sides. However, the appeal was quashed and building went ahead.

Although similar in style to Merrion Square, Fitzwilliam Square is smaller in scale, with sixty-nine houses as against ninety-five. The park is private, owned by the inhabitants of the square and other fortunate locals, but it can, nevertheless, be glimpsed, either through its enclosing railings (erected following an Act of Parliament in 1913) or through one of its four arched gates. It has a beautifully maintained garden with lawn, seats, pathways, spreading chestnut trees and a retaining border that includes many thriving hollies.

The majority of the houses on the square today are used as offices, chiefly for law and accountancy firms, but in the mid-nineteenth century they were identifiable mainly as the homes of members of the legal and medical professions.

During the 1890s Fitzwilliam Square Park was used to hold the Irish lawn tennis championships. At the time of the 1916 Rising, many houses were opened as emergency hospitals for soldiers. Later, in 1919, Eamon de Valera resided at No. 5, before setting off for the United States on a fund-raising mission for the nationalist cause.

Other well-known figures associated with Fitzwilliam Square are William Dargan (1799–1867), founder of Irish Rail and the National Gallery, who lived at No. 2 on the east side, and Robert Lloyd Praeger (1865–1953), botanist and author, who lived on the south side.

William Butler Yeats (1865–1939) stayed at No. 42 for a brief period in 1928, before moving to Rathfarnham, and Jack Yeats (1871–1951) lived at No. 18.

Not open to the public

Nearby: Iveagh Gardens, Merrion Square, St Stephen's Green, Grand Canal

---

Iveagh Gardens

A sumptuous splendour welcomes the visitor to the spacious, but secluded, Iveagh Gardens. The Gardens were designed between 1863 and 1865 by the landscape architect Ninian Niven for the International Exhibition of Arts and Manufactures held at Earlsfort Terrace in 1865, and are divided into three main sections which replicate Italian, North American and English styles.

The central parterre is embellished with statues, lawns and fountains. Its layout was inspired by the Bois de Boulogne in Paris, which was designed after the Italian style. The southern end of the Gardens, by contrast, has a more natural, North American flavour, with rocky outcrops. Next to it, a miniature maze copies that found in London's Hampton Court. There is also an archery lawn.

This eight-and-a-half-acre parcel of land, between Earlsfort Terrace and Harcourt Street, has had several names since the mid-eighteenth century, including Leeson's Fields, Clonmell's Lawns and Coburg Gardens. Each name signifies a change in ownership of the grounds. The most colourful owner was John Scott, Earl of Clonmell. Scott, by profession a judge, was a notoriously debauched scoundrel and was nicknamed 'Copper-Faced Jack' because of the ruddy complexion which resulted from a life of dissipation in the company of his pal, Buck Whaley, the flamboyant rake and gambler. Today, a nightclub in Leeson Street is named after Buck Whaley, while Copper-Faced Jack's in Harcourt Street perpetuates Lord Clonmell's memory.

On Scott's death, the eight and a half acres were, for a brief time in 1817, leased to the public, at which time they became known as 'Coburg Gardens'. Later, in 1823, a road was planned to go through the land, but that never materialized. The Gardens remained intact, and in 1862 Benjamin Lee Guinness, Lord Iveagh, purchased them, at which stage they acquired their present title.

In 1863 Lord Iveagh leased the Gardens to the Dublin Exhibition Palace and Winter Garden Company, who then organized an exhibition at Earlsfort Terrace. A building was specially constructed for the event and it is, today, the only purpose-built Victorian exhibition building still standing in Dublin. (Its façade was redesigned, in 1918, by R.M. Butler.) It now houses the National Concert Hall and UCD's Faculty of Medicine.

The Exhibition was opened on 9 May by the then Prince of Wales. The opening was a splendid social occasion with choirs and military bands. Handel's 'Coronation Anthem' and Mayerbeer's 'Grand March' from *Le Prophète* were performed, and a ball was given by the Lord Mayor at the Mansion House.

Among the many exhibits, a section on 'Machinery in Motion' featured a steam-pumping engine, which not only heated the building but also operated the Gardens' lawn sprinklers and cascades. This exhibit was the out-

come of a growing interest in technology, paralleled, socially, by an awakening desire for greater communication between different classes of society.

The Show's Directors, leading patrons and businessmen including the Duke of Leinster, Lord Talbot, Lord Iveagh and William Dargan, were of the opinion that exhibitions such as this would provide the perfect forum for class interaction as well as the practical education of the less privileged, a concept which may well have marked the origins of Ireland's present technical and vocational education schemes.

The exhibition building was sold in 1883 to the Commissioners of Public Works, to house the newly formed

Royal University (now incorporated with UCD). The Gardens, however, reverted to the Guinness family, and it was not until 1939 that they were presented to UCD, and, at last, became reunited with the Earlsfort Terrace building. In 1991 the Gardens passed into the custodianship of the Office of Public Works, and they are now tended by Dúchas.

Currently, Dúchas is implementing a programme of restoration which includes the repair of fountains and cascades and statue-lined walkways. On completion, the Iveagh Gardens will stand as one of the finest ornamental parks in Europe.

Opening hours:
March–October 8.00 until dark Monday–Saturday
February & November 8.00–17.00 Monday–Saturday
December–January 8.00–16.00 Monday–Saturday
(Sunday & Bank Holidays 10.00 until hours listed above)

Nearby: National Concert Hall, St Stephen's Green, Fitzwilliam Square, St Kevin's Park

---

St Stephen's Green

The fulfillment in 1880 of Sir Arthur Guinness's lifelong dream to open St Stephen's Green to the public had a defining impact on the character of the city. Located in the centre of Dublin, it is one of the best-tended and largest public parks (twenty-two acres) in Europe.

Part of the splendour of the park arises from its rich diversity of landscape features, including an ornamental lake and waterfall, lawns, and neat flower gardens, all surrounded by paths and comfortable seating bays. There is, too, an abundant collection of birds (geese, mallards and moorhens); trees (fifty species); and sculptures. A Garden for the Blind has labels on shrubs and herbs in braille.

St Stephen's Green occupies a site that was once part of an open marshy common extending to some sixty acres and used for sheep grazing. In 1663 Dublin Corporation decided to develop the land for residential use around a central, set-aside twenty-seven-acre Green, which was subsequently enclosed. Ninety building allotments were tendered by ballot to leading citizens, with a proviso that they would each plant six sycamores close to the wall and dyke surrounding the Green.

The west side of the Green, on which the Royal College of Surgeons stands, remained undeveloped until the mid-nineteenth century. Its unattractiveness stemmed from the fact that it had been a place of public executions. (A Bishop of Waterford, John Atherton, was executed there for bestiality in 1640.) It also bordered the poorer part of the city, known as the Raparee Fields, home of pickpockets and thieves. It was, as well, close to what was then a leper house in Lower Mercer Street, after whose adjoining chapel, 'St Stephen's', the Green takes its name.

In contrast to the west side, by the end of the eighteenth century the north, south and east sides of the Green were highly fashionable. On the south side, Sir Benjamin Guinness owned Nos 80 and 81, known as Iveagh House, a property bequeathed in 1936 to the Government, and now headquarters of the Department of Foreign Affairs. Buck Whaley, famous rake and gambler, son of Richard Whaley, priest-hunter and chapel-burner, lived at No. 85 (built 1765). This building was taken over as the Catholic University of Dublin in 1854, and is now known as Newman House by virtue of the fact that Cardinal Newman was Rector of the University. On the south side of the Green, Kerry House, once occupied by the Marquis of Lansdowne, has since 1824 been incorporated into the main body of the famous Shelbourne Hotel.

The Fusiliers' Arch, erected in 1907 at the Grafton Street entrance, is a memorial to the men of the Royal Dublin Fusiliers killed in action in the Boer War of 1899–1900. A bust of Countess Markievicz (1868–1927) honours a woman who was powerful and prominent in both the arts and republican circles around 1916. There is also a fine bust of the poet James Clarence Mangan (1803–49).

Opening hours: Monday–Saturday 8.00 until dark
Sunday & Bank Holidays 10.00 until dark

Gardens open Christmas Day 10.00–13.00

Nearby: St Stephen's Green Shopping Centre, Gaiety Theatre, Shelbourne Hotel, Iveagh Gardens, Fitzwilliam Square, Merrion Square

Grand Canal Park

O commemorate me where there is water
Canal water preferably, so stilly
Greeny at the heart of summer ...
—Patrick Kavanagh, 'Lines Written on a Seat
on the Grand Canal'

Dublin has two canals, the Royal and the Grand, to the
north and the south of the Liffey respectively, creating
waterway boundaries between the inner and outer city.
The Grand Canal features three city sections. The first is
Ringsend Basin, where the canal joins the Liffey and
flows into the sea. The second is the Circular Line, which
flows from Maquay Bridge, near the Waterway Visitors'
Centre, to Kilmainham. Lastly, the Dublin stretch of the
Main Line extends from Griffith Bridge to Hazelhatch.

The Circular Line, which circumscribes the southern
end of the city centre, has fourteen bridges, but featured
here is the area between Upper Mount Street and Portobello bridges, because it is the most attractive stretch of

the canal and contains several interesting cultural and historical features.

At Upper Mount Street, within sight of Huband Bridge, can be found St Stephen's Church. It was built in 1821 by John Bowden in the Greek-Revival style and bears the nickname 'The Pepper Canister' because of its octagonal, 100-foot-tall belfry tower and cupola. It closes the vista of the southern side of Merrion Square very pleasantly, and today, although still used for Church of Ireland services, the building has also become a venue for classical concerts and other events. Huband Bridge, named after Joseph Huband, one of the directors of the Canal Company, is possibly the most frequently painted of the canal bridges.

The next bridge, at Baggot Street, is officially named Macartney Bridge. Perhaps the best-known and most popular of the bridges, the area around it is particularly pretty. Patrick Kavanagh lived at a number of addresses in the area, among them 62 Pembroke Road, from 1943 to 1958. For him, the canal was a way of life. It was both his regular haunt and an inspiration for his poetry, and it was his wish to be commemorated with 'just a canal-bank seat for the passer by'. Accordingly, the great man is now honoured by a canal-bank seat and a bronze cast of himself, seated in contemplative pose, by the sculptor John Coll. An empty space on the bench lures the visitor to sit and share with Kavanagh the experience of the canal's magic.

Another bench at Baggot Street is dedicated to Percy French (1854–1920), who lived at 35 Mespil Road. French, an artist, engineer and songwriter, wrote the famous songs 'Are Ye Right There, Michael?' and 'The Mountains of Mourne'. His memorial seat was erected by the Waterways section of the Office of Public Works in association with Oliver Nulty of the Oriel Gallery, and bears the inscription, 'Remember me is all I ask, and yet if the remembrance prove a task, forget.'

Between the next two bridges, Eustace and Portobello respectively, Harcourt Terrace can be found. Sarah Purser (1848–1943), the well-known painter, lived at No. 11 between 1887 and 1909. No. 4 was home to Micheál MacLiammóir and Hilton Edwards, co-founders of the Gate Theatre.

The nature-lover may be interested to note that, along this stretch of water, a pair of swans have been regularly nesting for some years, close to the tow-path.

The original purpose of the canals, in the days of poor roads and before the railways, was to provide passenger and cargo transport. The Grand Canal was constructed between 1756 and 1803, and it thrived until the arrival of the railways in 1829. In 1834 faster 'fly' boats were introduced for passenger traffic. These boats were towed at speed by either two or four horses. Four horses at a gallop could pull a ninety-passenger boat at ten miles per hour, an improvement on the previous rate of four miles per hour.

The service operated out of the passenger terminus at the Grand Canal Hotel (built 1807, now Portobello College) on Portobello Bridge. However, the 'flies' were not sustainable competition for the rail service and by 1852 all passenger boats had been withdrawn, although the cargo boats were, at this stage, still operational.

In 1911 the Swedish Bollinder semi-diesel engine was introduced to replace the horse-drawn fleet. The Grand Canal Company was the first in the world to use this engine. However, during the Second World War a scarcity of fuel meant that horse-drawn barges were reinstated. In 1950 the canals and railways were amalgamated under one transport company, CIE, and in 1960 the last cargo boats were withdrawn.

It was at this stage that consideration was given to converting both canals into roads. Instead they were transferred to the Office of Public Works, under the Canals Act, 1986. Since 1996 the minister for Arts, Heritage, Gaeltacht and the Islands has had responsibility for the care, management and development of the canals for navigation, fishing and public recreation.

The Grand Canal has now been restocked with one hundred and seventy thousand fish, among them perch, carp, pike and bream, while tow-paths are currently

[97]

being developed as long-distance walking paths, with bank and hedgerow vegetation reflecting the habitat needs of aquatic invertebrates, hedgerow animals and birds.

It is hoped that, through this regeneration project, the canal will provide a regular resource for leisure activities such as boating, fishing and walking, and its ageless tranquillity, so much admired by Kavanagh, will be safeguarded for the enjoyment and inspiration of future generations.

Opening hours: never closes

GRAND CANAL VISITOR CENTRE
June–September: 9.30–18.30 daily
October–May: 12.30–17.00 Wednesday–Sunday

Last admission 45 minutes before closing

Admission charge: Adult £2.00
Groups & Senior Citizens £1.50
Child/Student £1.00
Family rate £5.00

Nearby: St Stephen's Church

Dartmouth Square Park

Twenty minutes' walk from the city centre, Dartmouth Square is in a predominantly residential area of Dublin 4, off Upper Leeson Street. It is memorable because of its red-brick, three-storeyed terraced houses with their arched porchways at the top of granite steps, typical of late nineteenth-century Victorian architecture.

The land on which Dartmouth Square was built had originally been low-lying and was intersected by two streams. Until around the mid-nineteenth century a solitary house, thought to have been a nursery, had stood beside the Grand Canal. A Mr Darley owned the land and Rathmines Urban District Council records show that, in 1896, he sold it to them for use as a dump. The accumulated rubble later served to raise the level of the land for building purposes.

Dartmouth Square was the last nineteenth-century square to be developed in Dublin. Uxbridge Terrace was the name given to the first row of houses (numbers 1–17) built on the west side, from Dartmouth Road to the

canal. The north, south and east sides followed. Initially, the Square was known as 'Uxbridge Square', but later the name 'Dartmouth Square' was adopted.

Following the construction of the square, the central area was leased by Loreto College as a sports ground, and it was not until nearly a century later, in the 1980s, that it was acquired by Dublin Corporation for conversion into a park, with full public access. During the landscaping process, bottles of various shapes and sizes, which had constituted part of the landfill, were upturned by the Parks Department, bringing an archaeological dimension to the project.

The park has been designed to reflect its immediate Victorian environment. Its lawns are adorned with a pergola and neat box hedging, which typify the ornamentation prevalent at the end of the nineteenth century.

Well-known figures who lived in Dartmouth Square are the actor Barry Fitzgerald, who won an Oscar for his part in 'Going My Way'; Frank Duff, founder of the Legion of Mary, who lived at No. 51 from 1921–7; Luke Kelly of the Dubliners, who lived at No. 7; and Paul Durcan, the poet, who was born at No. 57 in 1944.

Opening hours: every day during daylight hours

Nearby: Burlington Hotel

Herbert Park

They had walked on towards the township of Pembroke and now, as they went on slowly along the avenues, the trees and the scattered lights in the villas soothed their minds. The air of wealth and repose diffused about them seemed to comfort their neediness.

—James Joyce, *Ulysses*

Named after Sidney Herbert, Lord Pembroke (1809–61), this park can be found between the U.S. Embassy and the Royal Dublin Society in Ballsbridge, an opulent area which, with its tree-lined terraces of red-brick houses, wears the charming air of Victorian respectability.

There's a bright spectral magic about the pergola with its ceiling, matted like a bird's nest – a tangle of leaves, roots and twigs, with ivy fronds cascading down the sides. Horse chestnut trees lining the lake reflect their own glory in the water. Along one side of the pergola, in summer, a wide herbaceous border displays bright perennials – red-hot pokers, yellow daisies, lemon mint, pampas grass and fig bushes, all sumptuously overgrown.

In fact, the pergola and the lake are the only two features remaining from the great International Trade Exhibition, which was held here in 1907. This was visited by King Edward VII of England, and exhibitors from all parts of the British Empire were represented at it. The pergola had been the verandah for the Fine Arts building, and the lake had been used in the Canadian exhibit – a waterchute.

The land on which the park stands was first opened to the public in August 1911, and it boasts a variety of fine trees – lime, beech, birch and Norway maple. A sample of the latter was planted in 1977 by the mother of the

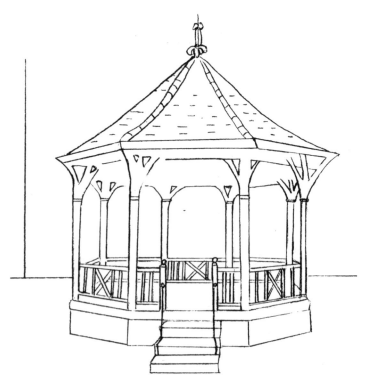

then President of the United States, Jimmy Carter. There are also samples of hornbeam, planted to commemorate Ireland's first National Tree Week in 1985. (The hornbeam is often mistaken for either the elm, because of the similarity of its leaves, or the beech, because of its smooth grey bark.)

There are, too, a number of species of bird, including wood pigeon, chaffinch, dunnock and robin; and ducks, namely moorhen, coot and mallard. The lake has been plentifully supplied with carp since 1978 by the Fisheries Board, in conjunction with Dublin Corporation.

This large park, approximately twenty-seven acres in extent, has numerous amenities, including three tennis courts, a croquet lawn, bowling green, Gaelic football pitch and soccer pitch.

Opening hours: every day during daylight hours

Nearby: Royal Dublin Society

Belgrave Square Park

In wet weather Belgrave Square Park can become water-logged, for one of Dublin's underground rivers, the Swan, with its source in Kimmage Manor, runs through Rathmines, and a tributary, rising in Garville Avenue, flows right underneath the park. So, after heavy rain, pools of water tend to gather on top of the ground along the river line. However, the wetness of the park has not decreased the popularity of the Square over the years as an attractive place to live.

Sculptor Joseph Watkins (1839–71), known for his modelling of many well-known people, including Charles Dickens, lived at No. 49; Patrick J. Smyth, of Young Ireland fame, lived at No. 15; and George Francis Savage Armstrong, author of 'Stories of Wicklow' and other poems, lived at No. 57.

James Joyce (1882–1941) lived nearby at No. 23 Castlewood Avenue for a short period as a child, from 1884 to 1887. His brothers Stanislaus and Charles were born here, and in Joyce's *Ulysses* a character named Margaret Cummins of No. 32 Castlewood Avenue marries Alfred H. Hunter in Rathmines Church on 1 February 1898. (In real life, a Mrs Anne Cummins lived at No. 32 Castlewood Avenue.) Walter Osborne (1859–1903), the painter, lived at No. 5 Castlewood Avenue with his wife Anne. He is known for an ability to capture the vagaries of light in homely domestic scenes, for example, 'The Dublin Park – Light and Shade', of 1895, or 'The House Builders', of 1902.

Belgrave Square was developed in 1851. The east side was the first to be constructed. The other three sides swiftly followed and the name 'Belgrave Square', chosen by Mr Hugh Morrison, a speculator who had developed much of the south side, was soon adopted by all. The park until this time had been known as Church Fields, because it was situated east of the Holy Trinity Church. It was waste land and was used as a right of way to Milltown.

Once the park had been created, agreement was not easily reached over its enclosure, which is why today only part of it is railed in, while the remainder is – more economically – walled in. Like a discarded toy, the grounds became neglected by the Square's residents, and remained an overgrown and weedy liability until The High School, established at 40 Harcourt Street in the 1870s, began in the 1890s to use the park as its camogie pitch. Thus it remained, being used also by other local schools for rugby and cricket, until the 1970s, when The High School moved its premises to Zion Road, Rathgar, and no longer needed the grounds.

Currently, Belgrave Square Park is under the custodianship of Dublin Corporation. With pathways, seating areas, shrubbery borders, lawn, and an abundance of newly planted tree saplings, it has become an attractive asset to the area.

Opening hours: every day during daylight hours

Nearby: Swan Centre Shopping Mall

Palmerston Park

Crescent-shaped Palmerston Park has become a bird haven, with nesting boxes that have attracted siskins, chaffinches, greencrests, and tree creepers, while sparrow hawks nest in the park's tall pines.

The park was created in 1892 out of three and a half acres of land that had been part of Lord Palmerston's estate in Upper Rathmines. It was not enclosed, however, until 1893, because of a dispute as to whether or not a road should run through it.

As one of the three Dublin parks designed by William Sheppard (the other two being Harold's Cross Park and St Stephen's Green), it has the distinct Sheppard style, exemplified by combining the formal with the natural, and by the presence of a waterfall and pond, characteristics which give a different look from, say, the well-manicured Merrion Square. Among its trees are examples of both deciduous and coniferous varieties, including copper beech, chestnut and cedar. It also boasts a splendid magnolia tree.

The shelter in Palmerston Park, another Sheppard feature, has a six-foot by four-foot lean-to adjoining it, which, before the construction of the official detached gardeners' premises, was the only private accommodation the gardeners had access to. The story goes that on one occasion as many as thirteen fitted into it for a Christmas meal.

Most of the houses on the park were built in the 1870s and 1880s. Several are associated with famous names. At No. 3, later Mount Temple School, once known as Miss Sweeney's (circa 1926), Elizabeth Yeats gave painting lessons to children, including two who were to grow up to be artists, Melanie and Louis Le Brocquy.

No. 20 is the Museum of Childhood, run by Madame Mollereau. It was at the house named 'Griablah' in Palmerston Park that, in 1931, the formation of An Oige, The Irish Youth Hostelling Association, was planned by Terry Trench, whose family home it was.

The residents of Palmerston Park have been fortunate in that it has always been on a public transport route. The last horse-drawn tram travelled there in 1910, and from then until the buses took over there were electric trams, marked first by a white circle, then by a No. 12. Now the Nos. 13, 14 and 14A buses go to the park from the city centre, an easy twenty-minute journey for anyone wishing to experience the country in the town.

Opening hours: every day during daylight hours

Buses: 16 or 16A from O'Connell Street

Harold's Cross Park

In 1968 Hurricane Charlie uprooted one of this park's lime trees. Fortunately, there was no further major damage and today the park offers a variety of both deciduous and coniferous trees, from horse chestnut to cedar.

The name 'Harold's Cross' was coined in the fifteenth century, when the Archbishop of Dublin's land extended to this area from the inner city. A cross was erected here to delineate the boundary of church land, in the hope of preventing encroachment onto it by the 'Harolds', or 'outlanders', who lived beyond the Archdiocese, in the vicinity of Whitechurch.

What today is parkland was then merely a Green, and the area around it was rural, dotted sparsely with a few huts. In time, however, the hamlet grew into a village and, during the eighteenth century, Harold's Cross became a desirable neighbourhood, being recommended for its fresh air, and considered suitable both as a summer retreat and for invalid convalescence. At that time, two pubs close to the Green, the Cat and Bagpipes and the

Cherry Tree, offered local entertainment, while the Royal Oak and the Old Grinder's Joy were popular inns.

For many years a May Sports Day was held annually on the Green, and each May Day there was dancing around a maypole. This activity was stopped, however, in the mid 1800s, following a veto by the local Poor Clare nuns.

The Green, the centre for open-air festivals, was also the site of public punishments; in 1798 rebels were publicly flogged here. It was only in the late 1800s that the park's use as a public gathering place was terminated. This move was provoked by Dublin's first unemployment protest meeting, attended by some three thousand five hundred people. The outcome was a march to the Mansion House for talks with the Lord Mayor, who conceded that the opportunity to work should be a realistic option for all who wanted it.

After that, in 1894, the Green was harnessed into an enclosed triangular, three-acre park, to suit the suburban ethos of the Rathmines Township Commissioners. It was opened to the public on 1 May 1894, by a Mr Edward Fottrell, the Commissioners' Chairman. Like St Stephen's Green, it was designed by the landscape architect William Sheppard, and bears the marks of his distinctive style – a blend of the formal and the informal, with the characteristic inclusion of a pond and shelter.

In the mid-1930s Dublin Corporation took over the upkeep of the park. Today it is a well-tended garden, comprising lawns, trees, pathways and shrubbery borders. It is home to many species of bird including dunnocks, robins, sparrows and greencrests, who particularly enjoy the pond.

There's a children's play area, too, and a Supervisory Schools Nature Study Programme uses the park as a facility to encourage nature awareness in the young. In this vein, a Rose Garden, containing Peace Roses, was planted in 1994 by a local group of girl-guides, to commemorate the hundredth birthday of their founder, Lady Baden-Powell.

A commemorative cross, erected in 1954, pays tribute to the surviving members of the 4th Battalion Dublin Brigade IRA. It is in memory of all who served with it since Easter 1916.

Opening hours: every day during daylight hours

Nearby: Museum of Childhood, 20 Palmerston Park (01 4978696)

Rathfarnham Castle Park

This four-acre park, which enhances the stately Castle of Rathfarnham, is the fruit of a restoration project by South Dublin Corporation, which parallels that by Dúchas to restore the Castle.

The park consists of an extensive lawn and a woodland area with a small stream and man-made lake. The stream's water is piped through the grounds of Beaufort College and under the road near the Yellow House pub (opposite the castle) from a tributary of the River Dodder, the Owendore. The lake is the habitat of Chinese geese as well as various species of duck.

An area of grassland and gravel surrounds the Castle, which was built in 1583 (possibly on the site of an earlier castle) for Adam Loftus, a rich Yorkshire man, who settled in Ireland and held several positions of power, including Archbishop of Dublin, Lord Chancellor of Ireland, and first Provost of Trinity College.

During its Elizabethan phase, the castle was more a fortified house, with exterior defensive features including four arrow-shaped flanking towers, whose purpose was the early detection of hostile intruders (such as the marauding Byrnes and O'Tooles from the Wicklow hills).

Rathfarnham Castle remained the Loftus family seat until 1724, when it was sold to pay off gambling debts. Mr 'Speaker' Conolly, owner of Castletown House, bought it, but discovered he preferred his more up-to-date Castletown, and let Rathfarnham Castle to tenants. During this time the process of the Castle's eighteenth-century remodelling began.

The property reverted to the Loftus family in 1767, and Henry Loftus took over the refurbishment work. His intention was to convert it into a comfortable Georgian home. Accordingly, the interiors of the castle were squared off, columns were erected and multi-light sash windows were added, while Portland stone was imported from Dorset to create a luxurious hall floor. Sir William Chambers and James 'Athenian' Stuart, two of the leading architects of the day, were commissioned to work on the building, which is the only site in Ireland or Britain where their work can be seen together.

The ceiling in the lobby of the Castle is magnificent, while the 'Gilt Room' displays a sumptuous ceiling by Stuart, and depicts symbols of eight Greek gods.

Henry Loftus, who died childless in 1783, was succeeded by his nephew, Charles Tottenham, but his family lost interest in Rathfarnham Castle and returned with most of the furniture and paintings to Loftus Hall in Co. Wexford and Castle Hume in Co. Fermanagh, so that by 1825 the castle was described as 'lately deserted'.

It was not until the early twentieth century that Rathfarnham Castle underwent further major remodelling, when, following a brief period of ownership by the Blackburne family, who also modified the building to suit their needs, it was sold to the Jesuits in 1916.

Under the new dispensation a stark functionality replaced the classical splendour for which the Castle had been known since the late eighteenth century. With their architect, Charles Pugin-Powell, the Jesuits erected wings to the north-west and south-west flankers to provide extra accommodation. They converted the ballroom into a chapel, and the windows of the bow of the ballroom were altered to fit stained-glass panels by Harry Clarke. Scenes from the life of Christ, painted by Patrick Tuohy, were installed in the drawing-room to replace the secular art attributed to Angelica Kauffmann.

By the mid 1980s the Jesuits no longer required such extensive accommodation, and decided to dispose of the property. Thus the Castle's fate changed course yet again. In 1986, in response to public concern over its future, it was declared a National Monument and the first phase of the present conservation work began.

Since 1986, the roof has been repaired, the twentieth-century wings have been removed to reveal the original defensive character of the building, the kitchen has been restored, structural repairs have been carried out and essential services have been provided. Research and analysis to conserve and restore interior and exterior finishes is currently in progress.

Capsule information overleaf.

Opening hours:
June–September 10.00–18.00 daily
October 10.00–17.00 daily
Easter Weekend 10.00–17.00
April 10.00–17.00 Sundays only
May 10.00–17.00 daily

Telephone 6613111 for winter opening hours.
Last admission 1 hour before closing.

Access by guided tour only.

Admission:
Adult £1.50
Group & Senior Citizen £1.00
Child/Student 60p
Family rate £4.00

Buses: 16, 16A from O'Connell Street; 47, 47A, 47B from Hawkins Street; 17 (Blackrock - Rialto); 75 (Dun Laoghaire-Tallaght)

Nearby: Yellow House pub, St Enda's Park, Marley Park

St Enda's Park

Sometimes my heart hath shaken with great joy
To see a leaping squirrel in a tree,
Or a red ladybird upon a stalk,
Or little rabbits in a field at evening,
Lit by a slanting sun.
—Patrick Pearse, 'The Wayfarer'

St Enda's Park in Grange Road, Rathfarnham, is the home of the Pearse Museum. It covers roughly forty acres and contains many natural attractions, including an artificial lake, the Whitechurch stream, wooded areas and open glades. There's also a walled garden, and a courtyard with a Nature Study Room housing nature awareness exhibits and informative displays on aspects of the flora and fauna to be found within the grounds.

Patrick Pearse was born in 1879 at No. 27 Great Brunswick Street (now Pearse Street) in central Dublin. The son of an English stone-carver and an Irish mother, he was influenced from an early age by his maternal great-aunt Margaret, who, through her telling of Irish folktales, kindled in him a love of the Irish language and its lore.

Pearse's passion for the Irish language coincided with an upsurge of the Gaelic League movement dedicated to its revival. In 1903 Pearse became editor of the organization's bi-lingual newspaper, *An Claidheamh Soluis* (The Sword of Light). He subsequently made a study of bi-lingualism in Belgian schools. In 1908 he set up his own bi-lingual school at Cullenswood House, Ranelagh, naming it St Enda's, after St Enda of Aran who had abandoned the herioc life of a warrior to teach a devoted band of scholars in the remote seclusion of the Aran Islands.

Pearse disapproved of the official education system in Ireland at the time, which he referred to as 'The Murder Machine', because its repressive spirit destroyed the individuality of both teacher and pupil. He therefore established an independent system at St Enda's, aimed to produce upright citizens of character and individuality.

Pearse believed that 'education has not to do with the manufacture of things but with the fostering and growth of things', and the teacher–pupil relationship was based on that of 'fosterer' and 'foster-child'. He believed, too, that pleasant surroundings stimulate inspired achievement, and nature study was an important part of the school's curriculum.

In 1910 St Enda's was transferred from Cullenwood to The Hermitage, a gracious house with extensive grounds close to the base of the Dublin mountains.

Perhaps appropriately, the estate had historical associations which appealed to Pearse's idealistic and nationalist sensibilities. Built in 1780 on land originally known as the 'Fields of Odin', The Hermitage had been the home of a Dublin dentist, Edward Hudson, whose son, William

Elliot Hudson, was a supporter of the Young Ireland movement. William was also an Irish-language enthusiast, and had donated his collection of books and manuscripts to the Royal Irish Academy, together with £500 towards the publication of an Irish dictionary.

The estate also had associations with Robert Emmet. Emmet and Sarah Curran, who were friends of the Hudson family, used to meet in secret in the grounds of The Hermitage because Sarah's father, John Philpot Curran, a famous lawyer who lived in the nearby Priory, frowned upon their relationship. This romance was, however, tragically curtailed in 1803 when Emmet was executed for leading a brief, ill-fated rebellion.

Emmet's association with The Hermitage is remembered today by a tree-lined avenue which bears the name 'Emmet's Walk' and leads to 'Emmet's Fort', which was a trysting place for the young lovers.

Pearse's passion for Ireland's language and culture eventually spilled over into the active political arena, culminating in the Easter Rising of 1916. Pearse was executed for his role in the Rising on 3 May, his brother Willie on 4 May, in Kilmainham Gaol.

Following Pearse's death, financial difficulties and declining enrolment dogged St Enda's College, which was eventually closed in 1935. However, the property remained in the possession of the Pearse family until 1969. The house and grounds then passed into state care, and today they are maintained by Dúchas.

Capsule information overleaf.

Opening hours:
PARK:
November–January 10.00–16.30 daily
February–March 10–17.30 daily
April & September–October 10.00–19.00 daily
May–August 10.00–20.00 daily

MUSEUM:
November–January 10.00–16.30 daily
February–March 10–17.30 daily
April & September–October 10.00–19.00 daily
May–August 10.00–13.00, 14.00–17.30 daily

Last admission 45 minutes before closing.

Buses: 16 from O'Connell Street. Turn off Grange Road into car park at terminus.

Guided tours around Pearse Museum available on request. Audio-visual presentation: 'This Man Kept a School'. Facilities include well-presented Nature Study Centre, self-guiding trail, toilets, car/coach park. Outdoor concerts during summer season. Telephone: (01) 493 4208 (Pat Cooke) Fax: (01) 493 6120